THE ULTIMATE GUIDE TO HUNTING™

INSIDER TIPS FOR WING SHOOTING

XINA M. UHL AND
JENNIFER BRINGLE

rosen publishing's rosen central®

New York

Published in 2019 by The Rosen Publishing Group, Inc.
29 East 21st Street, New York, NY 10010

First Edition

Library of Congress Cataloging-in-Publication Data

Names: Uhl, Xina M., author. | Bringle, Jennifer, author.
Title: Insider tips for wing shooting / Xina M. Uhl and Jennifer Bringle.
Description: New York : Rosen Central, 2019. | Series: The ultimate guide to hunting | Includes bibliographical references and index. | Audience: Grades 5–8.
Identifiers: LCCN 2017048464| ISBN 9781508181927 (library bound) | ISBN 9781508181934 (pbk.)
Classification: LCC SK313 .U35 2018 | DDC 799.2/4—dc23
LC record available at https://lccn.loc.gov/2017048464

Manufactured in the United States of America

CONTENTS

INTRODUCTION

Hunting has been practiced around the world for thousands of years. Meat gained from the hunt allowed people to feed their families, both in the past and today. Furs and skins are used to make clothing and shelter, and bones, antlers, and other parts are used for ornamentation. While there are still some people who practice subsistence living, requiring them to hunt in the absence of obtaining meat from grocers, most people in modern day North America do not need to hunt in order to survive. Still, hunting remains one of the most popular sports on the continent for millions of people. Hunters represent a sizable market for guns, archery equipment, and other, specialized supplies and equipment. Dogs are popular aids and companions for hunters, too. They require training, veterinary care, and more.

In 2011, the U.S. Fish & Wildlife Service found that Americans spent $33.7 billion on hunting, with $14 billion of that going toward equipment and $10.4 billion going toward hunting trip expenses. The same survey found that 13.7 million people went hunting; 1.5 million of them hunted pheasants, and 1.3 million hunted doves.

Game animals, including deer and birds, may not be available in stores. And while hunting for food and sport are powerful motivators, other reasons figure in as well. Hunters may pursue pests that harbor disease, ruin crops, and endanger other animals. Sometimes animals become overpopulated, stressing the habitat they are a part of to the point where they may die of starvation if their numbers aren't reduced.

Hunters must follow the law since these laws are designed to protect animal populations from overhunting and to protect the

Hunting is often thought of as a male sport, but in recent years more women are enjoying the activity.

environment they live in. These laws involve designating hunting areas and hunting seasons, which are designed to ensure that animals are not overhunted or underhunted.

There are many different types of hunting, from big and small game to migratory birds and wing shooting, or shooting game birds in flight. Another name for wing shooting is upland hunting, as the birds being hunted are called upland birds. Wing shooting requires special skills because the target is moving, often at high speeds, through midair. Small birds such as doves, pheasants, grouse, chukar (also called chukar partridge), and prairie chickens make up many of the game birds wing shooters pursue. Hunters use shotguns and sometimes archery equipment and dogs to hunt these birds.

Before venturing out into the field, though, hunters must obtain the proper hunting licenses and permits from their state. Each state has its own rules and licensing requirements, and it's up to the hunter to be aware of those rules and regulations.

Hunter safety courses are an important part of that licensing process since hunters must learn the proper procedures for hunts, not to mention gun and weapon safety. Safety should be a hunter's number-one concern, since lives hang in the balance.

CHAPTER ONE

LEARNING ABOUT HUNTING

Hunters come in all shapes and sizes in many different location, but they all have one thing in common, and that is a need for the proper weapon and equipment. While there are many kinds of firearms used for hunting other animals, for wing shooting, the most commonly used weapon is the shotgun. Shotguns appropriate for wing shooting are over-unders, semiautomatics, and the upland shotgun.

The double-barrel over-under has two barrels stacked on top of each other, instead of side-by-side. A semiautomatic automatically loads—instead of having the action manually operated by a pump or lever, the action automatically cycles each time the shotgun is fired, ejecting the spent shell and reloading a fresh one into the chamber. The upland shotgun has side-by-side double barrels that are shorter than the average shotgun. Shorter barrels allow fast movement and easy maneuverability, which is essential for shooting fast-moving birds.

Wing shooters also often opt for lighter-weight guns. This is because wing shooters have to do quite a bit of walking when looking for the right hunting area. The downside of having a lightweight shotgun is that it is harder to control than a heavier one. With a lighter gun, the gun's swing momentum can cause the gun to get out of control. Hunters using lightweight guns must have strong body strength and control in order to keep a handle on their guns.

There are several different shotgun gauges. Common shotgun gauges are 10 gauge, 12 gauge, 16 gauge, 20 gauge, and

Shotguns are the recommended weapons for wing shooting. They come in different styles, and those designed for wing shooting have shorter barrels.

28 gauge. The smaller the gauge number, the larger the shotgun bore, or opening in the barrel. Gauge is determined by the number of lead balls of size equal to the approximate diameter of the bore that it takes to weigh one pound. For example, it would take 12 lead balls with the same diameter as a 12-gauge shotgun bore to weigh one pound. The .410-bore shotgun is the only exception to the gauge designation for shotguns. It has an actual bore diameter of 410/1000ths of an inch, which is approximately equivalent to a 67½ gauge.

Each gauge of shotgun shoots only shells of the same gauge. For example, 12-gauge guns use only 12-gauge shells. The gauge of a shotgun is usually marked on the rear of the barrel, and the gauge of a shell is marked on the shell as well as on the factory box.

LEARNING THE BASICS

One of the most important aspects of hunting is education. Just as drivers must take driver education

IMPORTANT SAFETY RULES TO REMEMBER

- Always point the muzzle of a firearm or a bow and arrow in a safe direction. Never point it toward yourself or another hunter.
- Treat every firearm or bow with the same respect you would show a loaded gun or nocked arrow. Even if a hunter thinks a gun or bow is unloaded, he or she still needs to be very careful.
- Be sure of the target and what is in front of and behind the target.
- Unload and safely store firearms or unstring conventional bows when not in use.
- Handle firearms, arrows, and ammunition carefully. They are weapons that can cause serious injury or death, and should be handled with extreme caution.
- Know your safe zone-of-fire and stick to it. Stepping out of a safe shooting zone can put the hunter, as well as other hunters, in danger of accidents.
- Wear hearing and eye protection when shooting. Guns can be very loud, and since it's so close to the body, the volume of the gun can cause hearing loss. Guns can also sometimes fly back toward a hunter, or shells being expelled from the gun can fly into a hunter's face, so it's important to make sure the eyes are protected with hunting glasses.

Safety should always be your first priority. This woman is wearing safety glasses, ear protection, and a flourescent vest.

courses, hunters must take hunting education courses before they are able to obtain a hunting license. Hunter education is incredibly important as it teaches hunters how to hunt safely, ethically, and legally.

Each state and Canadian province offers hunter education courses. Mandatory requirements differ by state or province. But, in general, most hunter education courses are taught according to standards established by the International Hunter Education Association (IHEA). These courses cover hunting safety, firearms, bows, wildlife identification, wildlife management, survival, game care, ethics, responsibility, and regulations.

Hunting safety is one of the most important aspects of hunter education courses. Basic hunting tips include the following: Tell someone where you will be hunting. If you get injured or lost, someone should be aware of your location. Avoid hunting alone.

This pheasant hunter is carrying her weapon in the recommended way for safety, pointed down.

If you must go alone, hunt in familiar areas. Dress properly. If it's cold, be sure to dress warmly enough to prevent hypothermia. If it's hot, be sure to wear lightweight clothing that will help prevent overheating. In sunny weather, sunscreen is a must since hunters spend long hours outside in the sun. A hat and protective eyewear are also good additions to a hunter's wardrobe.

Check your hunting equipment before every hunting outing. Make sure each gun or other piece of equipment works properly, and that you are familiar with the proper way to use it. Never carry a loaded weapon in a car or other vehicle. Be sure to unload guns when the hunt is finished. Wear enough hunter orange to make yourself visible to other hunters. A hunter orange hat or vest are good items to help make hunters stand out against the landscape. Wearing hunter orange is required in public hunting areas.

Be certain to hunt in designated hunting areas, and be mindful of the hunters around you. Make them aware of your presence to prevent accidents. Never drink or use drugs when hunting. Even if it's something as simple as cold medicine or cough syrup that could make you drowsy, you should never take it before hunting.

Finally, identify your target before shooting. Many hunting accidents and fatalities occur when hunters shoot before verifying their target. Use visual cues, listen for the bird's distinctive call, and look for flight patterns to verify that what you're aiming for is a bird. Identification also prevents accidentally shooting birds that aren't supposed to be hunted.

Traditional hunter education courses usually require attendance at multiple instructor-led sessions. Students must pass written and/or skills tests to pass the course. Some states offer alternative class formats for those whose schedules don't allow them to attend a traditional class. These alternative classes include at-home study through online classes, written manuals, CDs, DVDs, or videotapes. But students in these types of courses are still often required to attend some classes.

Generally, passing a hunter education course in one state or province will allow you to hunt in other states as well. Classes can be found either through state departments of natural resources, or through the IHEA's website.

SAFETY IS JOB ONE

In 2002, a young man hunting near Shelbyville, Texas, was having a remarkable hunting day. It was late afternoon when a deer walked out of the brush, right into his gun's range. He shot and bagged the deer, thinking how lucky he'd been. Then, a large buck stepped out, and right into his range again. Having bagged two deer, he couldn't believe his luck when he noticed movement in the brush again. It was nearly evening, but he decided to shoot one more time. He hit his mark, but instead of collecting another deer, he realized he'd made a horrible, tragic error—he accidentally shot a fellow hunter.

Knowing proper hunter safety procedures can mean the difference between life and death. Each year, hunters die or are injured unnecessarily because of the lack of good hunter safety practices.

In the Shelbyville case, both hunters made big mistakes that led to tragedy. The shooter shot before getting a good eye on his quarry, making it virtually impossible for him to identify his target. Since it was almost dark, this was even more true. He relied totally on sight, not bothering to listen for sound cues or check for behavioral or movement cues. And the victim neglected to wear enough hunter orange to stand out from the brush. Had he worn the proper orange attire, he might have been recognized as a person, rather than a deer.

Hunters must always put safety first when on the hunt. Knowing the proper safety procedures, and always following them, is essential to have a safe, enjoyable hunt.

CHAPTER TWO

RESPONSIBILITIES AND ETHICS

Although following the rules may be inconvenient sometimes, it is necessary when it comes to hunting. Breaking the rules and regulations can lead to harsh consequences for the environment, your quarry, and you and your fellow hunters. Rules are there for good reason.

LAWS AND REGULATIONS

Just as drivers must get a license before hitting the road, before going on a hunt most states require hunters to receive a hunting license or permit. The specific qualifications and regulations for these licenses and permits vary from state to state, but in general, a person must meet the following requirements before receiving a hunting license or permit:

- Minimum age requirement: Many states require hunters reach a certain age before they are able to receive a license or permit.
- Residency requirement: Most states require proof of residence in order to obtain a license or permit for that state. Other states will usually allow out-of-state hunters

to purchase licenses in their state, but they sometimes charge a higher fee for out-of-state hunters.

- Hunter safety requirement: Most states require hunters to take and pass a hunter safety course, and have proof of that, before obtaining a license or permit.

Wing shooting can be a difficult endeavor, involving careful preparation, concealment, and quick action at the right time.

Licensing and permit requirements and procedures vary by state. Contact your state's department of natural resources office or website to find out the specific rules for your state.

Once a hunter gets a license or permit, it's important they learn the proper rules and regulations of hunting, especially for the type of hunting they're doing. These rules and regulations vary from one type to another, depending on the animal being hunted, and the area where the hunting takes place.

One of the major regulations to follow when hunting is being mindful of legal hunting seasons. Hunting seasons are specific times of the year when hunters are allowed to hunt certain animals. These dates vary by state, and sometimes by region within the state. Hunting seasons help control the game population, and must be observed by hunters. Hunting outside the season is illegal. Hunters can find out the specific dates for hunting seasons by contacting their state department of natural resources.

Another major rule of hunting is to hunt only in areas where hunting is permitted. Trespassing on private property to hunt, or hunting in a preserve or animal sanctuary not designated as a legal hunting area is illegal. Hunters can be arrested for trespassing on private property, or for hunting in protected areas.

Not only that, trespassing can be dangerous. In designated hunting areas, hunters are aware there are others who may also be out there with them. They know to be mindful of other hunters. But in an area not designated for hunting, there's no guarantee that other people

ABOUT CLOSED SEASON

Although some hunters dislike it, closed season is a necessary element of hunting. The closed season allows proper wildlife management, and ensures that animal populations will remain high enough to make hunting possible.

For most hunting seasons, the main reason for closed season is reproduction. During peak reproduction times, game must be left to mate and reproduce in order to maintain the population. Without this regulation, populations would dwindle. This would make hunting difficult to impossible, and could even put animals in danger of extinction, at least in certain areas.

While some hunters might be tempted to ignore posted signs, they do so at their own peril.

Another reason for closed season particular to game birds and waterfowl is molting. At certain times during the year, birds molt, or shed worn and damaged feathers. New feathers grow in at the same time to replace these old feathers. Sometimes this can impair a bird's flying ability, which gives hunters an unfair advantage.

For hunters, it's important to always be mindful of hunting seasons, and to follow these rules. Hunting seasons make it possible for the sport to continue safely and fairly.

on the property will know you're there. This makes it a very dangerous situation, where someone could accidentally get hurt or even killed because they're in the wrong place at the wrong time.

Identification is another important thing to be mindful of when hunting, especially with birds. Because it's often hard to distinguish protected or illegal species from legal species simply by sight, using other methods of identification are necessary. Wing shooters must know flight patterns and characteristics, birdcalls, and habits to prevent shooting the wrong species by accident.

Hunters should also be aware of bag limits. These are limits on the number of animals a hunter may harvest and keep. In most cases, bag limits are imposed to prevent hunters from

The pheasants hanging here are waiting to be plucked, butchered, and prepared for delicious meals.

harvesting too many of a certain species, which could threaten the population size. Hunters who ignore or break these rules are called poachers.

Above all, it's critical to have consideration for fellow shooters. Make sure that you're aware of where they are, and they of you. Don't move around a lot, and try to avoid ruining their flight line. If you must pick up a bird, do so quickly, and get out of the way as soon as possible.

When wing shooting, there are many things to think about. It's important to take your time, be prepared, and make certain you follow all the necessary rules and regulations. This is the only way you can have a safe, legal, and enjoyable time wing shooting.

CHAPTER THREE

PLANNING AND PREPARING

Whether you are a beginning hunter or one who is experienced, it is essential to plan your trip well. Not only do you need to obtain the necessary permits and licenses to hunt, but you also need the best location, the best companions, and the proper equipment and supplies.

PRETRIP PREPARATION

Before planning a wing shooting trip, it's important to do a little pre-trip preparation. The first step is to figure out where and when you're going to hunt. Being aware of hunting seasons is the next step. Hunters must know when hunting seasons begin and end so they can plan their trip during the legal hunting season. Once a hunter knows when the season is open, he or she can plan the dates for the trip.

Another important thing to consider before planning a hunting trip is physical condition. Many people may not think about their physical condition before going hunting, but it's very important to avoid injury. Especially in wing shooting, hunters often have to do a great deal of walking to reach hunting spots, or to gather harvested game. It's important to be in good enough shape that

Wise hunters make sure they have the endurance and strength to meet the physical challenges of the hunt. That can mean regular trips to the gym.

walking long distances won't be a problem. In addition to walking, wing shooters must have good upper body strength to control their guns or operate a bow. If hunters don't have enough body strength to properly handle a gun or bow, they run the risk of hurting themselves or others.

In addition to strength and fatigue issues, hunters should always make sure they're healthy enough to hunt. If a hunter is sick and taking medicine those medications could impair judgment and make hunting dangerous. And if a hunter is sick, spending long hours outdoors and exerting energy to walk and use weapons can make them even more ill. It's important to be healthy and in good relatively good physical shape before going on a hunt.

Another important preparation for wing shooting is gaining a familiarity with bird behavior and habitats. This is essential for a number of reasons. First, it helps hunters find and identify game.

Second, it helps hunters distinguish the birds they're trying to hunt from those they are not.

Before a wing shooting hunt, many hunters like to get a little practice shooting their guns and working on their aim. A good

The scientific name for this beautiful pheasant is *Phasianus colchicus*. Latin or Greek scientific names are still used today.

way to practice for a wing shooting hunt is shooting skeet or clays. This is usually done on a shooting range. Clay discs are shot into the air by a machine, and hunters shoot at the discs. The discs fly through the air at high speeds, mimicking the speed of flying birds. Shooting skeet or clays can help hunters improve their aim and skill in shooting moving objects in the air.

ABOUT THE BIRDS

Once you know the types of bird habitats, you must find the areas where these habitats are common. There are many resources out there for finding hunting areas for particular types of birds. After you decide which states or provinces are best for hunting a particular kind of bird, you can then search local resources to find legal hunting areas.

Doves are most commonly found in open grassland and agricultural areas. Most states offer dove hunting. Doves aren't as prevalent in Canada, but they can be found and hunted in British Columbia and Quebec.

Pheasants thrive in a variety of land types. Grasslands, cropland, wetlands, and brush all provide habitats for pheasants. Iowa, Kansas, Minnesota, Nebraska, North Dakota, and South Dakota are some of the best states for hunting pheasants. Ontario, Alberta, and Saskatchewan offer good pheasant hunting opportunities in Canada.

Grouse live primarily in young aspen forests and brush land. When aspen isn't available, oak, lowland brush, and dense stands of trees are optional habitats. Michigan, Wisconsin, and Minnesota offer good opportunities for grouse hunting. Most of the Canadian provinces offer grouse hunting, as well.

Doves are the most numerous game bird in North America, with estimates topping 350 million. Hunters harvest more than 20 million each year.

Chukar flock to arid, mountainous, and rocky areas. They can be found in many western states. Oregon, Idaho, Nevada, and Washington all have plenty of good chukar habitat areas. British Columbia offers chukar hunting in Canada.

As their name implies, prairie chickens are mostly found living in prairie grassland in states such as Nebraska, Missouri, Kansas, and Oklahoma. They usually prefer undisturbed prairie with tall grass, but they can also be found in agricultural and prairie mixed land. Prairie chicken hunting is not as popular in Canada as it is in the United States, but it does occur in Alberta and Saskatchewan.

FINDING THE RIGHT SPOT

Once a hunter decides which states or provinces are best for the type of bird they want to hunt, the next step is locating legal hunting areas. One good resource for locating proper hunting areas is the state department of natural resources or state wildlife management agencies. These departments usually regulate hunting areas within a state, and helps enforce state hunting laws.

Public hunting areas are maintained by the government of the state where they are located. Hunters can find information about these areas from their state department of natural resources. Usually, the state provides pamphlets and websites offering information about public hunting areas. Information about public hunting areas and hunting regulations can be obtained where licenses are sold. Hunting in these areas is often free, or relatively inexpensive. That means they are very popular, which makes hunting on them a little more difficult because they can be crowded. But hunters can often obtain

This English pointer hunting dog is flushing a rooster pheasant out of his hiding place. Will the dog's master succeed in bringing down the bird?

maps to research the hunting area and possibly find lesser known spots.

Another good way of finding hunting areas is to contact local sportsmen's clubs. These clubs often own private hunting land that they allow nonmembers to hunt on for a fee. They also know the area and its hunting lands better than anyone, so they can advise hunters on which places to go to legally hunt. There are also a number of websites and hunting organizations that maintain hunting area databases online. With a little internet research, most hunters can quite easily find a good place for hunting.

The main thing to remember when choosing a location for a hunt is to be certain it's specified as an open hunting area. Hunters should never trespass on private land, or hunt in protected wildlife areas. Not only is this illegal and unethical, but it can also be dangerous.

When choosing a hunting area or preserve, there are several important things to consider. Find out what kind of facilities the preserve offers—practice shooting areas, skeet ranges, food, and lodging are all good amenities to look for. Ask about a preserve's dog policy. If hunters are allowed to bring their own dogs, find out if there are kennels in the event of an overnight stay. If the preserve provides dogs and guides, find out what kind of dogs they use.

Find out how you'll be hunting, be it on foot following a guide, from a four-wheel drive vehicle where you get out when the dogs go on point or even, in some regions, traditional mule-drawn wagons. Also, if fitness or agility is a concern, ask how much walking will be involved and check how rugged the terrain will be. Some preserves include extra ammunition in their fees. Ask if that's the case before leaving to hunt.

Certain states require different kinds of licenses and paperwork for hunting. Make sure the preserve can help you get the proper paperwork necessary to hunt in that state.

A standard preserve hunt includes two hunters with a guide. Find out if that's the case before going on a hunt—some preserves allow more than two hunters to hunt at the same time.

GUNS, AMMO, AND MORE

When planning a hunting trip, of course things such as guns and ammunition come to mind as items hunters must get and bring with them. But there are many other items hunters need while on a hunting trip.

One of the most important things to get for a hunting trip is the proper clothing. With wing shooting, hunters often do a lot of walking, sometimes over rough terrain. Because of this, it's critical to get a comfortable pair of shoes that offer plenty of support and traction. Finding shoes or boots that are waterproof is even better, as feet need protection from the elements while on a hunt.

Another important piece of gear for bird hunters is a vest. A vest provides the perfect place to store shot shells, a bottle of water, other gear, and your camera. Most good bird-hunting vests are orange to help hunters stand out to other hunters (except with dove hunting, which is a sit-and-wait hunt, where

CHECKLIST FOR THE HUNT

Before going on a hunt, it's a good idea to make a checklist to be certain to have everything you'll need. Here are some items to include on that list:

- **License/Permit. Make sure to have the proper license or permit in order to hunt legally.**
- **Proper Gun and Ammunition. Be sure to have the right gun for the type of hunting you'll do, and be certain to have enough ammunition for the gun.**
- **Hunting Gear. Always have the appropriate gear for a hunt—plenty of hunter orange (vest, jacket, etc.), comfortable shoes, shooting glasses, and a coat.**
- **Posthunt Gear: In the event of harvesting game, it's important to have a sharp hunting knife, plastic bags, clean cloths or paper towels, and a cooler filled with ice for dressing and transporting harvested game.**
- **Extra Gear: Be sure to have plenty of food, water, sunscreen, maps, and anything else you'll need to be safe and comfortable on a hunt.**

it's important for the hunter to blend in with his surroundings). And good vests also have a lot of pockets.

Many wing shooters also like to wear a hat with a brim while hunting. This shields the eyes from the sun, and helps hunters see better. Sturdy shooting glasses are another must-have for wing shooting trips. The best glasses protect hunters' eyes by wrapping around the face, without blocking a hunter's view. Ear protection is also important while hunting. Guns are very loud, especially when they're so close to the body while a hunter is shooting. Electronic earmuffs protect the ears from loud sounds, and also help hunters hear and locate their dogs.

A comfortable coat, particularly one that is waterproof, is also a good piece of gear to own. If it's cold out, or it rains, hunters need a good coat to keep them warm and dry. Along with a coat, wing shooters also sometimes like to bring soft leather gloves on a hunt. These protect the hands from the elements, and also help hunters hold their gun.

Another clothing item to consider for a wing shooting trip is brush pants or chaps to protect legs. These pants are specially made with rugged, tightly woven cotton to make them sturdy and able to protect legs from briars, twigs, and other prickly

Binoculars are a handy piece of equipment when scouting for birds. Although they are not necessary, they may make your hunting trip easier and more successful.

brush. Brush pants and chaps are also often made with a nylon layer or blend to give them additional sturdiness, and provide further protection from scratches. Some pants also include a Teflon outer layer to make them waterproof.

Other items hunters might bring on a wing shooting hunt include binoculars, a pair of hunting shears, and if they have a dog, an orange vest for their dog. Maps of the hunting area or a GPS unit are also helpful to prevent getting lost while hunting in unfamiliar areas. Sunscreen is good to bring on a hunt to protect skin against sunburn. And if a hunter will be out for a long time, it's also important to bring plenty of food and water to get through the day. Staying hydrated and fed will ensure the hunter stays healthy and able to hunt for as long as he or she pleases. But no matter what a hunter brings, he or she needs to be certain his or her clothing and gear are lightweight. A wing shooting hunter is likely to do a lot of walking, so it's important to have clothing and items that are easily portable and won't weigh the hunter down or unnecessarily fatigue him or her.

CHAPTER FOUR

ON THE HUNT

There's one item that can doom your hunt, and that is bringing the wrong gun for the type of birds and animals you are after. Think carefully about your choice of weapons, and be sure to get advice from experienced hunters and other experts.

For most wing shooting purposes, a shotgun is the best firearm for a hunt. The ideal shotgun for a wing shooting trip weighs around seven pounds (3 kg). Lengthwise, the shotgun shouldn't be more than four feet long (1.2 meters).

Choosing a gauge is also important. For wing shooting, the ideal gauge is 16. But these can often be hard to find, so a 20-gauge shotgun serves as a good alternative to a 16-gauge. The 20-gauge shotgun can handle pretty much any wing shooting fowl, offering the agility hit small, fast-moving birds from a distance.

Wing shooting is best done with a gun that shoots rounds very quickly. Reloading takes up valuable time and can cause a hunter to miss opportunities. But, it's important to remember that when shooting migratory birds, such as doves, it is illegal to have a gun that shoots more than three shells at a time.

In order to harvest birds, be sure to bring enough shotgun shells. Placing them in a handy belt can make them accessible during quick-moving events.

ABOUT BIRDS

Once a hunter chooses his gun, the next important issue to think about are hunting position and technique. When hunting different kinds of birds, hunters must use different positioning and technique.

QUAIL

Hunting quail has gotten a lot more difficult for hunters due to modern land use practices. The clearing of brush land in many states has made it difficult for quail to find habitat. And thus, it makes it difficult for hunters to find good quail hunting areas. Modern-day quail hunters must work harder to find quail "pockets," which are areas of brush cover where quail live.

Quail pockets can be very small sometimes, but a good hunter and his dog will check even the small spots, as these could yield good hunting. When hunting quail, hunters generally only need one dog, and the dog should move at a slow-to-moderate pace. When hunting these pockets, hunters should be careful to not overhunt one space. Harvesting one or two birds and then moving on to the next spot is the proper technique for responsible, ethical hunting.

DOVES

Concealment is the name of the game for dove hunting. Because these birds use their keen sense of vision to spot predators, dove hunters must try to blend in with their surroundings. Wearing camouflage is common practice in dove hunting. Adding camouflage tape or finish to your gun helps disguise it from doves. Also, some hunters use camouflage grease paint to minimize the shine on their faces.

Dove hunters scout potential hunting areas, usually with binoculars. Hunters should scout before 9 a.m. or after 3 p.m., when birds are more likely to be moving. Some good places to find doves are fields of just-harvested grain crops, near water bodies with wide areas of open mud along the shore, and gravely sites such as rural roads, sandbars, and gravel quarries.

Once a dove hunter finds a good location, he or she must stay put and try to blend into his or her surroundings as well as possible. A dove hunter must remain motionless until a dove gets within range, usually 25 to 35 yards (23–32 m).

GROUSE

A dog is a hunter's best asset in grouse hunting. An important thing to remember when grouse hunting with dogs is to hunt into the wind. This allows the dog to pick up scents more easily.

Grouse generally live in brushy areas, where there's a nearby food source. It's sometimes difficult to figure out where grouse will be, so experienced grouse hunters often keep a log of their hunts. This allows them to see patterns and predict where they'll be most likely to find the birds.

Grouse belong to the pheasant family. The Northern Hemisphere is home to eighteen species of grouse.

PRAIRIE CHICKENS

Prairie chicken hunters must search the tall grasses of prairie meadows bordering agricultural land to find their game. Dogs can help hunters sniff out the prairie chicken.

Prairie chickens are fairly predictable in their behavioral patterns, making it easy to hunt them if a hunter is willing to take the time to observe and note their patterns. For instance, they often visit the same fields and feeding areas, usually around the same time of day. An observant hunter can note this and be ready when the prairie chicken makes a move.

CHUKAR

Chukar prove to be a challenging bird for wing shooters to hunt. They often make their homes in rough terrain, making it physically challenging to access the areas where they are found. Chukar often live in rough, hilly areas. Although it may be the most strenuous option, climbing to the top of the hill may be the best plan for finding game. The chukar tend to stay on the higher elevations to offer easier escape from predators.

When hunting chukar, it's best to hunt with a dog, and stay moving with the dog. Chukar move quickly, so once a dog spots one, the hunter needs to be at the ready in order to harvest the bird.

Once a hunter shoots a target, obviously the next step is locating and bagging it. But sometimes, that's easier said than done. Birds naturally blend into their surroundings, so when they fall back into the brush, it can almost seem as if they've disappeared. Having a dog on the hunt certainly helps, but there are some other techniques hunters can use to make sure they find and collect all harvested birds.

The chukar partridge was introduced to North America as a game bird. This species has inhabited the Great Basin and southern Canada since the 1940s.

BEST PRACTICES

When a hunter gets a good shot, it's a natural instinct to want to rush over and collect the bird. But a hunter must fight that instinct and take a moment to stay put and observe his surroundings. This is important because no matter how obvious the fallen bird's position may seem, it may not be in the exact location a hunter thinks. But taking a moment to mark their position helps a hunter to know where to base their search from, and return to that spot to wait for the next bird. But also do not waste a lot of time marking position. It's very important to get to the bird quickly in case it wasn't fatally hit. A hunter doesn't want to leave a bird to suffer, or escape and die later, which would be wasteful.

A good signal to help hunters find downed birds is feathers floating in the air above the spot where the bird fell. A puff of feathers generally signals a solid hit. But, hunters must be aware of wind when looking for feathers—the wind can move the feathers away from where the bird actually fell.

Listening is another good technique for locating a downed bird. Chances are, the bird will still be moving after it has been shot, even if it's a clean shot. So, hunters should listen for movement in the brush to located their target. Hunters should not shoot birds on the ground.

When searching for a downed bird, hunters should widen the search in tight circles beyond the spot they think the bird fell. Hunters should also check tree and bush branches if they cannot find their quarry on the ground. It may have gotten tangled in the limbs or leaves of a tree or bush as it fell to the ground.

Hunters should mark their shooting spot to allow them to walk the shot line of where they were standing and where the bird may have fallen. Trail tape is good for marking the shot area, as is throwing down your hunting cap.

THE HUNTER'S BEST FRIEND

One of the greatest assets to a wing shooting hunt is a dog. Generally, wing shooters choose pointers and spaniels as their hunting dogs. These dogs rely on their sense of smell to find and point out game birds. Spaniels and pointers share many traits that make them ideal for wing shooting—powerful sense of smell, stamina, intelligence, affinity for water, speed, and courage. Additionally, these dogs are generally outgoing, well-mannered, and friendly, making them perfect for hunts.

At ground level, dogs detect things humans typically miss. In tall grasses, cornfields, and woods, it's best to let

Labrador retrievers were bred to be gun dogs, and they are specially skilled to retrieve pheasants. Owners must still train the dogs to get the results they want, though.

(CONTINUED ON THE NEXT PAGE)

(CONTINUED FROM THE PREVIOUS PAGE)

the dog follow his nose. Once he finds a scent and points out a spot, then the hunter can move forward.

When hunting on a preserve with a guide and his dogs, it's best for hunters to avoid interfering with the handler and his dogs. These dogs are used to working with their handler, and can respond to hand signals, whistles, and voice commands that only the handler and dog know. These dogs are trained to obey only their handlers, so attempting to command them is pointless and detrimental to the hunt. Even if a hunter wants to just pet the dog, he or she should always ask the handler first.

When hunting with dogs, it's important to be aware and careful not to shoot below eye level. Just as hunters must look out for themselves and other hunters, they must be careful for the safety of their dogs.

HUNTING IN A GROUP

While many wing shooters prefer to hunt alone, or with maybe one other person, group hunts are common in wing shooting. Especially on preserves, larger groups of hunters, often led by a guide and his dogs, is the common form of wing shooting hunts.

Many of the same rules apply to individual hunts and group hunts. But group hunts present a special set of rules and etiquette to follow. Before going on the trip, hunters should check with the rest of the group to be certain there's not a dress code. Some groups require hunters to wear a certain amount of hunter orange, or certain types of gear. If there is a dress code within the group, it's important for all hunters to follow.

Another important aspect of group hunts is dogs. Before going on the trip, the group should all be aware of who's bringing dogs, and how many. Hunters should all be prepared to hunt with them.

Safety when hunting with a group is extremely important. Because there are more people, and sometimes more dogs, it's critical for hunters to be aware of fellow hunters and their dogs at all times. These safety tips will help wing shooters be safe in a group hunt setting. Stay in line with other hunters. Do not get ahead or behind other hunters. When swinging through a shot, do not point or fire the gun in the vicinity of fellow shooters. Always be aware of your surroundings. Be careful of dogs when shooting. Do not rush the shot or shoot below eye level. If your gun is an autoloader, be sure to get a guard to prevent ejecting shells from hitting fellow hunters or their equipment.

In addition to safety considerations, hunters must follow special etiquette when participating in a group hunt. When choosing shots, hunters shouldn't go for a bird that might make a better target for another hunter. It's important to choose shots carefully. Along those same lines, hunters should strive for clean shots each time. Not only is this helpful to other hunters, it's the humane and ethical way to hunt.

Another thing to keep in mind is general behavior on a group hunt. Excessive talking or being loud is rude and detrimental to other hunters. And staying together is another key rule to remember when hunting with a group. If one member wanders off and becomes separated from the group, it can waste valuable hunting time trying to find him or her. In addition, it's dangerous to wander off from the group because it's easy to get lost or hurt. And if one member gets lost or hurt, it may take a long time to find the person.

CHAPTER FIVE

THE END OF THE HUNT

Once you have successfully harvested game, your next step is to transport and dress it. If you mean to eat the game you've harvested, it is essential that you follow the steps covered here. Preventing illness and injury are your top priorities.

HANDLING THE HARVEST

As a hunter begins to transport and dress his harvested game, he or she needs certain tools. A sharp hunting knife, resealable plastic bags, clean cloths or paper towels, and a cooler full of ice are essential. While still in the field, it's advisable to begin the process of dressing—preparing the game for eating—immediately. The first step is to remove the entrails—stomach, intestines, and so on. If there is food inside the bird, specifically grain or corn, it must be removed. Otherwise, the grain can ferment and ruin the meat. The heart and liver of many game birds can be used for giblets, which are the edible internal organs of a bird, often used in gravies. These must be stored in a plastic bag and kept clean and cold. Once the interior cavity of the bird has been cleared of entrails, wipe it down with a clean cloth.

If your hunt is successful, you will have a game bird or two like these to pluck, clean, and butcher.

Some states require hunters to make an identifying mark on birds to verify they are legal harvests. Birds may be plucked and skinned in the field. If this is the case, it's important to save the feathers in a plastic bag for identification purposes.

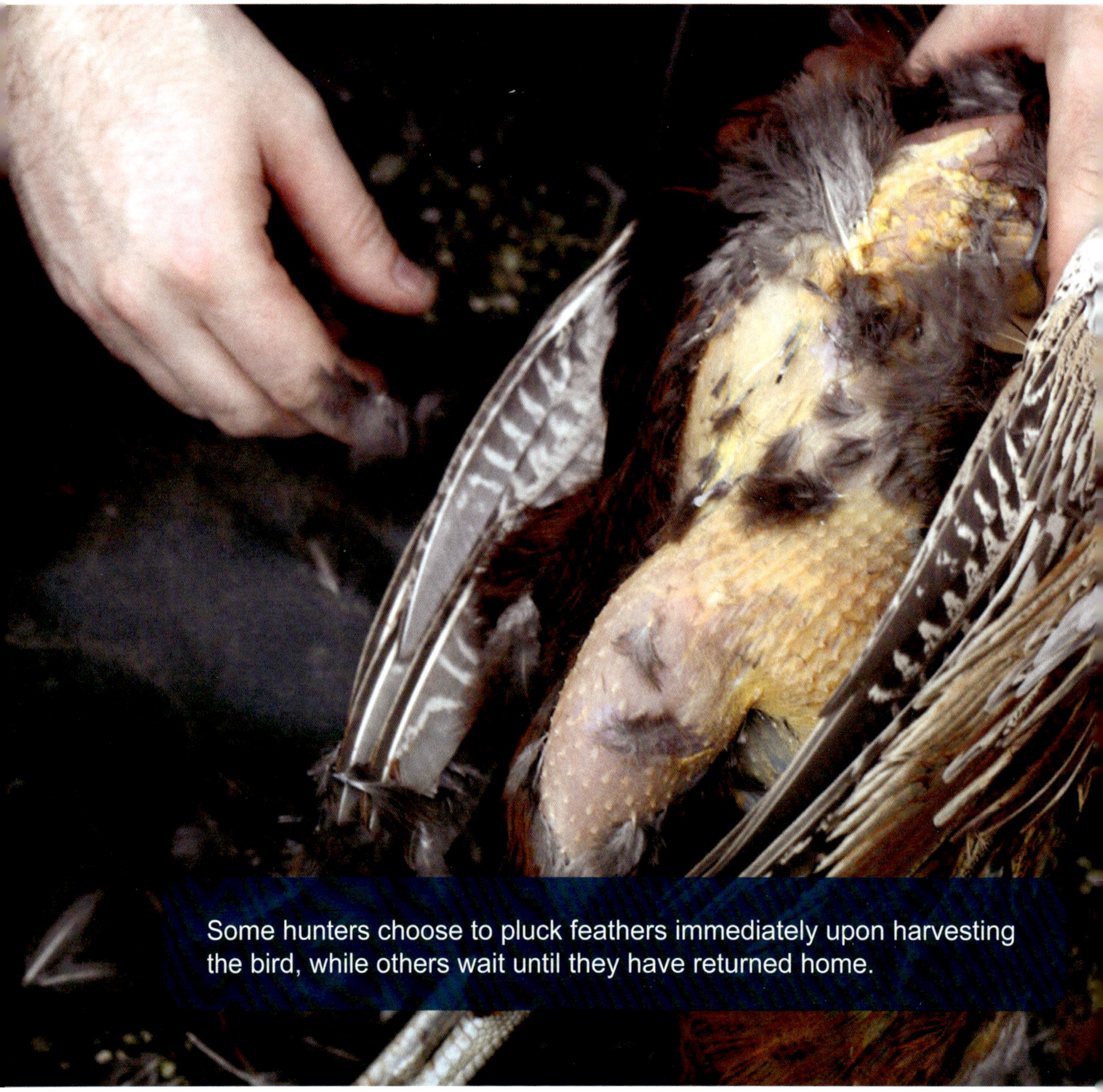

Some hunters choose to pluck feathers immediately upon harvesting the bird, while others wait until they have returned home.

It's very important to cool harvested game quickly. The birds should be placed in plastic bags and put on ice. This keeps the meat from being contaminated by bacteria, and it also helps the meat retain its flavor. Birds should not be piled on top of each other—there should be a little ice between each so that they cool properly. When putting the cooler into the car, it should be stored in the car's cabin, and not in the trunk. The trunk's enclosed space does not allow the heat to escape the birds as easily. And because of this, it's also important to keep the car cabin well ventilated.

DRESSING FOR SUCCESS

Once the birds are back home, they must be dressed. Hunters should wash hands, knives, and cutting boards or surfaces thoroughly with hot, soapy water before preparing the harvested game. If the bird hasn't already been plucked and skinned, it should be done at this time. Once the bird has been plucked and skinned, it should be soaked in cold water, often with salt added, for an hour or so to help remove excess blood.

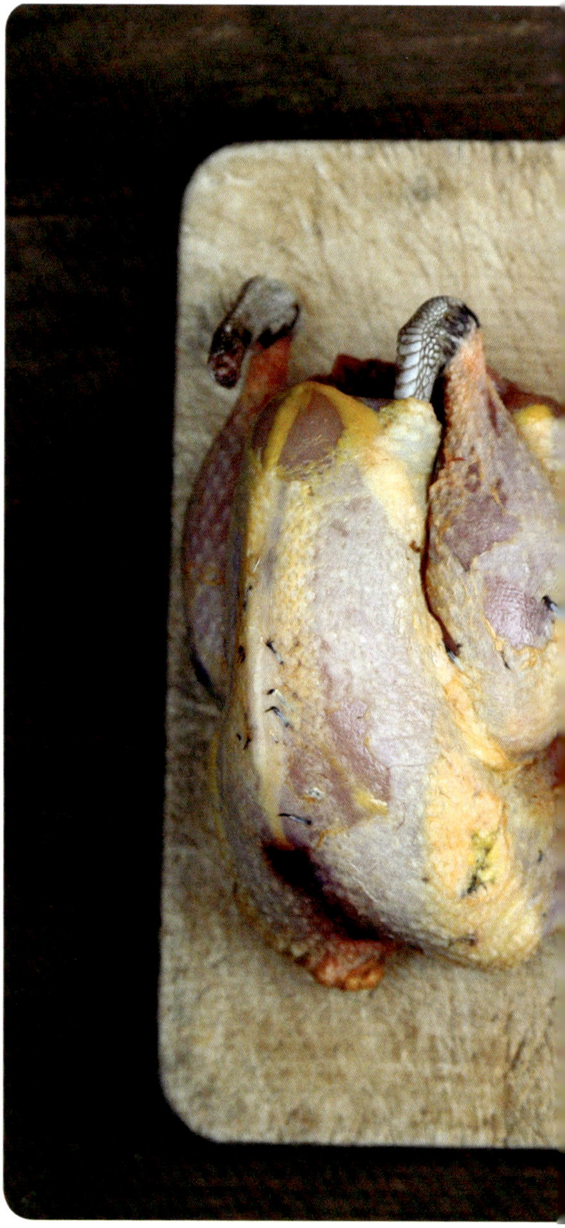

Once the excess blood is removed, hunters use knives to cut the game into useable pieces—breasts, drumsticks, and so on. If the meat will be eaten soon, it can be stored in the refrigerator. If it won't be eaten in the next couple days, the meat should be frozen to retain freshness and flavor. The meat should be wrapped tightly in freezer wrap or aluminum foil and then placed inside plastic freezer bags or stored in a freezer bag filled with water. Wrapping tightly is necessary to remove excess air from the package. It's important to label the meat with a date, as it should be used within a year of the hunt.

When preparing harvested game for eating, the age of the bird dictates how it's cooked. Different cooking methods apply for birds of different ages. A hunter can determine the bird's age by checking the beak, breastbones, and legs. Younger birds have flexible beaks, softer breastbones, and lighter legs. Older birds have inflexible beaks, brittle breastbones, and darker, hard-skinned legs. For younger

Depending on the age of the harvested bird, cooking methods may vary. Older birds require more moist heat.

birds, dry cookery methods such as frying work best. For older birds, moist cookery methods such as stewing or braising are the way to go.

TROPHY TERMS

While some people use the game they harvest for food, others choose to preserve their birds with taxidermy. Taxidermy is the practice of stuffing and mounting dead animals for display. Many people do this to preserve the birds they harvest, often displaying them in their homes and sometimes even in museums. Taxidermy is a fairly popular hobby in the United States and Canada.

The goal in taxidermy is to make the animal look as lifelike as possible. Harvested animals are generally frozen whole until the taxidermist is ready to prepare them. They then skin the bird and treat the skin with chemicals to keep it from decomposing. Then the taxidermist measures and poses the remaining muscle fibers and bones. He uses those measurements and the body to make a plaster mold. The mold is used to create the internal base of the body, and the treated skin and feathers are then placed over the internal base. Taxidermists sometimes use glass eyes and artificial teeth for mammals.

One of the key elements of making the bird look lifelike is posing. Many birds are posed to look as though they're in flight, displaying their wings. If a bird doesn't fly in nature, it's best to pose them standing. Regardless of how they are posed, birds preserved through taxidermy allow hunters to enjoy their hunt for years to come.

Many people say they don't like to eat wild birds because of the "wild" or "gamey" taste. A good way to minimize this is to be certain to trim off as much of the fat as possible. Another good

It may take some time to learn how to properly prepare roast pheasant, but the effort is rewarding, not to mention delicious.

method for reducing this, and helping the meat maintain moisture is to wrap it in bacon. When cooking harvested game, the most important thing to remember is to make sure the meat is thoroughly cooked. The internal temperature of the meat should be at least 165 degrees Fahrenheit (74 degrees Celsius). The juices should run clear, and no pinkness should remain in the meat.

GLOSSARY

bore Opening in the barrel of a shotgun.

chukar A grayish-brown Eurasian partridge; an upland bird in the pheasant family.

cover A brushy or grassy area used by birds for shelter and hiding.

dove A small, wild pigeon.

dressing Skinning, plucking, cutting up, and preparing a bird/animal for eating.

entrails Internal organs including the stomach and intestines.

ethics Moral principles governing behavior and obligations.

fowl Another name for birds.

game Wild animals hunted for food and sport.

gauge A standard measurement.

giblets Edible internal organs of birds, including the heart, liver, and gizzard.

grouse Small, reddish-brown ground dwelling bird.

habitat The environment where an animal normally lives.

mandatory Necessary.

migratory Traveling from place to place.

muzzle The open end of a weapon from which a shot is fired.

nocked When an arrow is placed in notches on the bow in order to hold it steady to shoot.

opt Choose.

pheasant Large, long-tailed wild bird.

prairie A treeless, grassy plain area.

prairie chicken Large, henlike grouse bird that lives in North American prairie lands.

preserve An area where hunting is permitted during certain months.

skeet The sport of shooting at clay pigeons that are hurled upward in such a way as to simulate the flight of a bird.

subsistence The minimum amount of food needed to remain alive.

taxidermy The act of preserving and mounting dead animals for display.

trespassing To enter private property unwanted or unauthorized.

upland hunting An American term for a form of bird hunting in which the hunter pursues upland birds including quail, pheasant, grouse, chukar, and prairie chickens.

wing shooting Shooting game birds that are flying.

FOR MORE INFORMATION

Canadian Wildlife Service (CWS)
Atlantic Region
Environment and Climate Change Canada
17 Waterfowl Lane, PO Box 6227
Sackville NB E4L 1G6
Canada
(800) 668-6767
Website: https://www.canada.ca/en/services/environment/wildlife-plants-species/migratory-birds.html
The Canadian Wildlife Service is the national wildlife agency handling wildlife matters that are the responsibility of the federal government.

International Hunter Education Association
800 East 73rd Avenue, Unit 2
Denver, CO 80229
(303) 430-7233
Website: http://www.ihea-usa.org
Facebook and Twitter: @InternationalHunterEducationAssociation
The International Hunter Education Association (IHEA) is the professional association for sixty-seven state and provincial wildlife conservation agencies and the seventy thousand volunteer instructors who teach hunter education in North America.

National Rifle Association of America
11250 Waples Mill Road
Fairfax, VA 22030
(800) 672-3888
Website: http://www.nra.org

Facebook and Twitter: @NRA
Instagram: @nationalrifleassociation
The National Rifle Association of America provides firearms education and advocacy throughout the world.

Natural Resources Canada
580 Booth
Ottawa, ON K1A 0E4
Canada
(855) 525-9293
Website: http://www.nrcan-rncan.gc.ca
Twitter: @NRCan
Natural Resources Canada champions innovation and expertise in earth sciences, forestry, energy, and minerals and metals to ensure the responsible and sustainable development of the nation's natural resources.

National Shooting Sports Foundation (NSSF)
Flintlock Ridge Office Center
11 Mile Hill Road
Newtown, CT 06470-2359
(203) 426-1320
Website: http://www.nssf.org
Facebook: @nssfcomm
Twitter: @NSSF
Instagram: @thenssf
The National Shooting Sports Foundation (NSSF) is the trade association for the shooting, hunting, and firearms industry. Formed in 1961, NSSF is a nonprofit organization that promotes, protects, and preserves hunting and the shooting sports.

U.S. Fish & Wildlife Service
1849 C Street NW

Washington, DC 20240
(800) 344-9453
Website: http://www.fws.gov
Facebook/Twitter/Instagram: @usfws
The mission of the U.S. Fish & Wildlife Service is to work with others to conserve, protect, and enhance fish, wildlife, plants, and their habitats for the continuing benefit of the American people.

USDA, NRCS, Office of the Chief
1400 Independence Avenue SW, Room 5105-A
Washington, DC 20250
(202) 720-7246
Website: http://www.nrcs.usda.gov
Facebook: @usda
Twitter: @usda_nrcs
NRCS works with landowners through conservation planning and assistance designed to benefit the soil, water, air, plants, and animals that result in productive lands and healthy ecosystems.

FOR FURTHER READING

Bjorklund, Ruth. *Migratory and Resident Birds Explained*. New York, NY: Cavendish Square Publishing, 2017.

Boy Scouts of America. "Shotgun Shooting." Irving, TX: Boy Scouts of America, 2016.

Carpenter, Tom and Bill Sherck. *Pheasant Hunting*. Minneapolis, MN: Sportszone, 2016.

Cashin, John. *Firearms Safety.* Pittsburgh, PA: Eldorado Ink, 2014.

Gaspar, Joe, and Jack Weaver. *Hunting*. New York, NY: Rosen Publishing, 2016.

Hemstock, Annie. *Hunting Laws and Safety*. New York, NY: Rosen Publishing, 2015.

Llanas, Sheila Griffin. *Common Pheasant.* Minneapolis, MN: ABDO Publishing, 2014.

Meyer, Susan. *Hunting Dogs: Different Breeds and Special Purposes*. New York, NY: Rosen Publishing, 2013.

Milner, Robert. *Absolutely Positively Gundog Training: Positive Training for Your Retriever Gundog*. CreateSpace, 2015.

Nickens, T. Edward. *The Best of The Total Outdoorsman: 501 Essential Tips and Tricks.* San Francisco, CA: Weldon Owen, 2017.

BIBLIOGRAPHY

Bowlen, Bruce. *The Orvis Wingshooting Handbook, Fully Revised and Updated: Proven Techniques for Better Shotgunning*. Guilford, CT: The Lyon's Press, 2008.

Brant, Alex. *The Complete Guide to Wing Shooting: The Ultimate Handbook to a Specialized Sport.* Guilford, CT: The Lyon's Press, 2005.

Casada, Jim. Wingshooting USA. "Getting Started (or Re-started) in Bird Hunting." http://www.wingshootingusa.org/Bird_Hunting_Library/Getting_Started.cfm.

Faw, Michael D. Wingshooting USA. "Geared for a Day Afield." http://www.wingshootingusa.org/Bird_Hunting_Library/geared.cfm.

Garden-Robinson, Julie, and Martin Marchello. "From Field to Table...A Pocket Guide to Care and Handling Game Birds." https://www.ag.ndsu.edu/pubs/yf/foods/fn537.pdf.

"Quick Facts." U.S. Fish & Wildlife Service. 2011. https://www.census.gov/prod/2012pubs/fhw11-qkfact.pdf.

Triplett, Todd. *The Complete Guide to Upland Bird Taxidermy: How to Prepare and Preserve Pheasants, Grouse, Quail, and Other Gamebirds.* Guilford, CT: Globe Pequot Press, 2006.

Williams, Ben O. *Wingshooting Wisdom: Prairie: A Guidebook for Finding & Hunting Public Lands.* Minocqua, WI: Willow Creek Press, 2006.

INDEX

ABOUT THE AUTHORS

Xina M. Uhl has written numerous educational books for young people, in addition to textbooks, teacher's guides, lessons, and assessment questions. She has tackled subjects including sports, history, biographies, technology, and health concerns. Although she has friends and family who hunt, she shoots animals only through her camera lens. Her blog details her publications as well as interesting facts and the occasional cat picture.

Jennifer Bringle grew up in a family of hunters in North Carolina. She has written several other books for children and teens on subjects such as homelessness, reproductive rights, and theater lighting.

ABOUT THE CONSULTANT

Benjamin Cowan has over twenty years of both big game and small game hunting experience. In addition to being an avid hunter, Cowan is also a member of many conservation organizations. He currently resides in west Tennessee.

PHOTO CREDITS

Cover Steve Oehlenschlager/Shutterstock.com; back cover Drakuliren/Shutterstock .com; pp. 4–5 (background) Outdoor_Media/Shutterstock.com; p. 5 Mitch Kezar /Design Pics/Getty Images; pp. 7, 17, 23, 36, 46 Adam Fichna/Shutterstock.com; pp. 8–9 fstop123/E+/Getty Images; pp. 10–11 Paul Briden/Shutterstock.com; pp. 12–13 aluxum/E+/Getty Images; pp. 18–19 Colby A Lysne/Shutterstock.com; p. 20 Carl Johnson/First Light/Getty Images; p. 21 Alex Sharp/Photographer's Choice RF /Getty Images; pp. 24–25 Olena Yakobchuk/Shutterstock.com; pp. 26–27 Andrew _Howe_E+/Getty Images; pp. 28–29 Dennis Jacobsen/Shutterstock.com; pp. 30–31 JMichl/E+/Getty Images; p. 34 Vasily Pindyurin/Getty Images; p. 37 Ingram Publishing/Getty Images; p. 39 Bildagentur Zoonar GmbH/Shutterstock.com; pp. 40–41 Morteza Nemati/Shutterstock.com; pp. 43, 47 Martin Harvey/Gallo Images /Getty Images; pp. 48–49 John Carey/Photolibrary/Getty Images; pp. 50–51 Lisa Barber/StockFood Creative/Getty Images; p. 53 Shaiith/Shutterstock.com.

Design: Michael Moy; Photo Research: Xina M. Uhl